A Gift for

_____

From

_____

Date

If My People . . .

Published in Nashville, Tennessee, by Thomas
Nelson. Thomas Nelson is a registered trademark of
Thomas Nelson, Inc.

All Scripture is from NEW KING JAMES
VERSION © 1982, 1992 Thomas Nelson, Inc. Used
by permission. All rights reserved.

Cover photo used by permission of Katie Ryan Ogle.

ISBN-13: 978–1–4041–8728–3
ISBN-13: 978-1-4003-2194-0 (with Display)

Printed in the United States of America

12 13 14 15 16 AP 5 4 3 2 1

www.thomasnelson.com

A 40-DAY
PRAYER GUIDE
FOR OUR
NATION

if MY
PEOPLE...

by
Jack Countryman

A Division of Thomas Nelson Publishers

THOMAS NELSON
Since 1798

NASHVILLE DALLAS MEXICO CITY RIO DE JANEIRO

Freedom Is Never Free

Throughout the history of our country, men and women have been called to make a great sacrifice and give their time and sometimes their very lives that we might enjoy freedom, liberty, and the pursuit of happiness. With every challenge we have faced, we have risen to defend the nation we love and cherish.

Today, we find ourselves facing many of the same challenges of our forefathers. We have been at war with those who wish to destroy our land and jeopardize our religious freedom for many years. We find ourselves at the crossroads of determining the direction of our country's future and the role of Christianity in our nation.

The devoted prayers of all Americans will impact the future direction of our beloved country. Our prayer is that this booklet will draw you closer to our heavenly Father as you commit yourself to pray for our country.

★ ★ God Bless America! ★ ★

Freedom has its life in the hearts, the actions, the spirit of men and so it must be daily earned and refreshed—else like a flower cut from its life—giving roots, it will wither and die.

—Dwight D. Eisenhower

The Power of Prayer

Since our nation's very first days, God's greatest movements in our midst have been fashioned and sustained by prayer, from the signing of our earliest documents, to our triumphs over days of darkness, to the spiritual awakenings that have sustained our faith and resolve over the centuries. Throughout Scripture and throughout our history as a nation, persistent, prevailing, intentional, and never-ending prayer has always brought the presence of God.

How vast are the possibilities when we pray! Prayer is a wonderful power placed by the almighty God into the hands of His saints. When we humbly seek His face in prayer, He is moved to act on our behalf and accomplish His desires for us.

And when we seek God in prayer for our leaders, we impact the very direction our nation will take. This forty-day prayer journey is designed to help quicken your prayers, to encourage you to seek God's will for our future and continually intercede on behalf of our nation. Prayerfully seek His face every day, believe that your prayers are making a difference, and claim all victory that is and is to come! For there is tremendous power in prayer.

DAY 1

★
★ ★

If My people who are called by My name will
humble themselves, and pray and seek My
face, and turn from their wicked ways, then I
will hear from heaven, and will forgive their
sin and heal their land.

2 CHRONICLES 7:14

Father,
We seek Your sovereign blessing on our
nation. Forgive us for our shortcomings
and the times when we have failed You.
Draw us back to Your love and strengthen
us as a nation to serve and honor You in
all that we do. May we forever be faithful
to the calling that You have given us. We
respectfully and humbly give thanks for
Your continued blessing.

Call to Me, and I will answer you, and show
you great and mighty things, which you do
not know.

JEREMIAH 33:3

Lord,
You have asked us to call to You, with the
promise that You will answer when we do.
We humbly seek Your guidance for our
nation. Give us wisdom so that we will be
a people guided by Your Spirit and filled
with Your presence. Help us, O Lord, to
honor You in word and deed, that we as a
people will have Your blessing and favor.

DAY 3

Be anxious for nothing, but in everything by prayer and supplication, with thanksgiving, let your requests be made known to God; and the peace of God, which surpasses all understanding, will guard your hearts and minds through Christ Jesus.

PHILIPPIANS 4:6–7

Father,
The worries of each day are ever around us. Conflict, both within and without, threatens the peace we so desperately want and seek. Father, we come to You with open hearts, seeking Your guidance and being content with all that You have given us as a nation. Guard our hearts, O Lord, so that we will be faithful to You, and let the peace of Your presence surround us each and every day.

Now it shall come to pass, if you diligently obey the voice of the LORD your God, to observe carefully all His commandments which I command you today, that the LORD your God will set you high above all nations of the earth. And all these blessings shall come upon you and overtake you, because you obey the voice of the LORD your God: Blessed shall you be in the city, and blessed shall you be in the country.

DEUTERONOMY 28:1–3

Father,
Humble our hearts today so that we will hear Your voice. Help us as a nation to obey Your voice in all that we say and do. Continue to bless us, O Lord, and give us a compassionate and giving heart toward those around us. Hold us to a higher calling, that we will carefully observe Your commandments and be a nation under God with liberty and justice for all.

DAY 5 ★★

For I know the thoughts that I think toward
you, says the LORD, thoughts of peace and
not of evil, to give you a future and a hope.
Then you will call upon Me and go and pray
to Me, and I will listen to you. And you will
seek Me and find Me, when you search for
Me with all your heart.

JEREMIAH 29:11–13

Father,
We know that Your heart's desire for us
is to be at peace with You and with those
around us. Place within our hearts the
desire to live for You and to listen to the
leading of Your Spirit. Let us diligently
search for You. Open our eyes that we
might see what is good, honorable, and just
for this country and for the well-being of
all people.

George Washington

O eternal and everlasting God, . . . increase my faith in the sweet promises of the gospel; give me repentance from dead works; pardon my wanderings, and direct my thoughts unto thyself, the God of my salvation; teach me how to live in thy fear, labor in thy service, and ever to run in the ways of thy commandments; make me always watchful over my heart, that neither the terrors of conscience, the loathing of holy duties, the love of sin, nor an unwillingness to depart this life, may cast me into a spiritual slumber, but daily frame me more and more into the likeness of thy son Jesus Christ, that living in thy fear, and dying in thy favor, I may in thy appointed time attain the resurrection of the just unto eternal life bless my family, friends, and kindred.

—Undated Prayer from
Washington's Prayer
Journal, Mount Vernon

DAY 6

★
★ ★

"Go therefore and make disciples of all the nations, baptizing them in the name of the Father and of the Son and of the Holy Spirit, teaching them to observe all things that I have commanded you; and lo, I am with you always, even to the end of the age."

MATTHEW 28:19–20

Lord,

You have commanded us to make disciples of all nations—may we begin within our own hearts! You are the way, the truth, and the life, and we thank You for Your promise to be with us always. Give us sincerity of heart and unfailing courage to spread this good news, whether with our neighbors across the street or with lost souls across the earth. We trust in You to work through us—without You we can do nothing!

"If you abide in Me, and My words abide in you, you will ask what you desire, and it shall be done for you. By this My Father is glorified, that you bear much fruit; so you will be My disciples."

JOHN 15:7–8

Lord,

We as a people have become self-absorbed and busy with activities that bring temporal value. Help us turn our hearts back to You and Your Word so our nation will bear the fruit of righteousness and be set above all other nations! Strengthen us with the power of Your Spirit in our inner being as we strive to abide in You and to continue in faith that You will do more for us than we could ever imagine.

DAY 8

Confess your trespasses to one another,
and pray for one another, that you may be
healed. The effective, fervent prayer of a
righteous man avails much.

JAMES 5:16

Father,

Give us Your guidance and strength as we honestly confess our sins to You and to one another. And give us compassionate hearts as we pray for each other and our leaders across the country and the world. Rid us of judgment, condemnation, and pride, and fill us with a spirit of grace, mercy, and love. Create in our hearts a fervent desire to pray every day for Your leadership to reign in our lives.

*The sacrifice of the wicked is an abomination
to the LORD,
But the prayer of the upright is His delight.*

PROVERBS 15:8

Father,
Your Word says that if we delight ourselves
in You, You will give us the desires of our
hearts (Psalm 37:4). Please direct our
paths in Your ways everlasting so that Your
will becomes our desire; so that Your way
becomes our delight. Fill us with the power
of Your presence and bind us together as
a people of one nation under God. And
through each day, to You be the glory for
all goodness and blessing that come our
way.

DAY 10

Rejoice always, pray without ceasing, in everything give thanks; for this is the will of God in Christ Jesus for you.

1 THESSALONIANS 5:16–18

Father,

The joy of the Lord is our strength; therefore, let us rejoice as a nation and as a people that have been blessed beyond all that we could ask or conceive. Let us pray each day for Your divine guidance, O Lord, and never forget Your benefits. Thank You, Lord, that You welcome us to Your throne of grace to receive Your blessing.

Thomas Jefferson

Almighty God, Who has given us this good land for our heritage; We humbly beseech Thee that we may always prove ourselves a people mindful of Thy favor and glad to do Thy will. Bless our land with honorable ministry, sound learning, and pure manners. Save us from violence, discord, and confusion, from pride and arrogance, and from every evil way. Defend our liberties, and fashion into one united people, the multitude brought hither out of many kindreds and tongues. Endow with Thy spirit of wisdom those whom in Thy name we entrust the authority of government, that there may be justice and peace at home, and that through obedience to Thy law, we may show forth Thy praise among the nations of the earth. In time of prosperity fill our hearts with thankfulness, and in the day of trouble, suffer not our trust in Thee to fail; all of which we ask through Jesus Christ our Lord. Amen.

—Washington, DC,
March 4, 1801

DAY 11

Likewise the Spirit also helps in our weaknesses. For we do not know what we should pray for as we ought, but the Spirit Himself makes intercession for us with groanings which cannot be uttered.

ROMANS 8:26

Thank You, Lord, for the gift of Your Spirit who continually helps us overcome our weaknesses. We confess that all things are possible through You and *nothing* is possible without You! Open our hearts and intercede with the Father that we may humble ourselves in Your presence. We thank You for Your forgiveness. Strengthen us to live with purpose and empower us to serve You.

The Lord is my rock and my fortress and my
    deliverer;
My God, my strength, in whom I will trust;
My shield and the horn of my salvation, my
    stronghold.
I will call upon the Lord, who is worthy to
    be praised;
So shall I be saved from my enemies.

PSALM 18:2–3

Lord,
You are the rock and strength of this
nation. You are the only one who can
deliver us from our enemies. We trust in
You and pray humbly for Your guidance
and direction for this great nation. Give us
wisdom to make right choices. Help us to
live in such a way that Your name will be
honored in all things. May You forever be
praised.

DAY 13

Evening and morning and at noon
I will pray, and cry aloud,
And He shall hear my voice.

PSALM 55:17

Father,
We exalt our praise and adoration to You
all throughout the day and night! May
we never forget that You are merciful and
gracious, and that You, our Creator, receive
our devotion and prayers with an atten-
tive, listening ear. Give us eyes to see the
splendor of Your holiness and ears to hear
the majesty of Your voice as You lead us to
holy and righteous living.

We give thanks to the God and Father of our
Lord Jesus Christ, praying always for you,
since we heard of your faith in Christ Jesus
and of your love for all the saints.

COLOSSIANS 1:3–4

Father,
We humbly come before You and ask
that Your Spirit reach across the lands to
all who are hurting and spiritually lost.
Restore their hearts with hope everlasting;
comfort them with Your tender, loving
arms. May we be sensitive to their needs,
whether physical or spiritual, and be eager
and willing to share Your love for them,
just as You have bestowed Your love upon
us.

DAY 15

And this I pray, that your love may abound still more and more in knowledge and all discernment, that you may approve the things that are excellent, that you may be sincere and without offense till the day of Christ.

PHILIPPIANS 1:9–10

Father,
May Your love flow through and around us. Speak to our hearts and open our minds that we may see You and the light of Your glory. Cleanse us, O Lord, that we may stand before You without blemish. Help us as a nation to be a discerning people with moral voices who will bring honor and glory to You, O God.

Abraham Lincoln

Fondly do we hope, fervently do we pray, that this mighty scourge of war may speedily pass away. Yet if God wills that it continues . . . until every drop of blood drawn with the lash shall be paid by another drawn with the sword . . . so still it must be said that the judgments of the Lord are true and righteous altogether. With malice toward none, with charity for all, with firmness in the right as God gives us to see the right, let us finish the work we are in, to bind up the nations' wounds, to care for him who shall have borne the battle, and for his widow and for his orphans, to do all which may achieve and cherish a just and a lasting peace among ourselves and with all nations.

—Second Inaugural
Address, March 4, 1865

DAY 16

For this reason I bow my knees to the Father of our Lord Jesus Christ, from whom the whole family in heaven and earth is named, that He would grant you, according to the riches of His glory, to be strengthened with might through His Spirit in the inner man . . . to know the love of Christ which passes knowledge; that you may be filled with all the fullness of God.

EPHESIANS 3:14–16, 19

Lord,

We bow before You in humble thanks-giving for Your gifts of power and strength, fortitude and might! We claim the riches of Your glory and the fullness of Your grace that come through the indwelling of Your Spirit within us. We pray for our nation to remain firm and steadfast in the knowl-edge of Your truth and the promise of the victory that is ours through Christ, who loves us.

I will sing to the LORD as long as I live;
I will sing praise to my God while I have my
being.
May my meditation be sweet to Him;
I will be glad in the LORD.

PSALM 104:33–34

O Lord,
We lift our voices and praise Your holy
name! May You forever be the center of
our thoughts, that in all things we may lift
You up in worship and song. Let the words
of our mouths and the meditations of our
hearts be a sweet aroma to You, for You
are our King—our joy comes from You!
Righteousness and justice are the foundation of Your throne; therefore we praise
Your holy name forever.

DAY 18

Give ear to my words, O Lord,
Consider my meditation.
Give heed to the voice of my cry,
My King and my God,
For to You I will pray.
My voice You shall hear in the morning,
       O Lord;
In the morning I will direct it to You,
And I will look up.

PSALM 5:1–3

We beg You, O Lord, to hear our supplications. Do not let our words fall on deaf ears. Let us come to You each morning with hearts full of joy, for You are our Most High God, and everything we have comes from You. Bless us that we might bless others. Let us always look to You for every provision. Let us each be an open vessel filled with Your wisdom, that others might know Your saving grace.

Hear me when I call, O God of my
*   righteousness!*
You have relieved me in my distress;
Have mercy on me, and hear my prayer.

PSALM 4:1

Father,
You are *so* wonderful! Through Jesus
Christ we have an open invitation to come
to You in prayer. We give thanks for this
blessing and each day find joy in all that
You give to us. What a blessed people we
are to know and embrace Your unconditional love.

DAY 20

The Lord has heard my supplication;
The Lord will receive my prayer.

PSALM 6:9

Father,
We thank You for hearing our petition.
Strengthen us by the power of Your Spirit
to live in such a way that glorifies You.
Forgive us when we do things that dis-
please You and separate us from Your
presence. Lead us each day, that we might
live lives that are pleasing to You. May You
forever be praised.

Franklin D. Roosevelt

Almighty God: Our sons, pride of our nation, this day have set upon a mighty endeavor, a struggle to preserve our Republic, our religion and our civilization, and to set free a suffering humanity. . . .

Lead them straight and true; give strength to their arms, stoutness to their hearts, steadfastness in their faith. . . . Their road will be long and hard. For the enemy is strong. . . . Success may not come with rushing speed, but we shall return again and again; and we know by Thy grace, and by the righteousness of our cause, our sons will triumph. . . .

With Thy blessing, we shall prevail over the unholy forces of our enemy. Help us to conquer the apostles of greed and racial arrogances. Lead us to the saving of our country, and with our sister nations into a world unity that will spell a sure peace—a peace invulnerable to the schemings of unworthy men. And a peace that will let all men live in freedom, reaping the just rewards of their honest toil.

—D-Day, June 6, 1944

Because Your lovingkindness is better than
*   life,*
My lips shall praise You.
Thus I will bless You while I live;
I will lift up my hands in Your name. . . .
Because You have been my help,
Therefore in the shadow of Your wings
*   I will rejoice.*

PSALM 63:3–4, 7

Father,
We praise You for Your grace, mercy, and
lovingkindness. May we as a nation look
to You with thanksgiving in our hearts for
the blessings You have poured upon us. Let
us forever rest in the shadow of Your wings
and shout for joy with praise, for You are a
most gracious God, and You bless us even
beyond our understanding.

Hear my cry, O God;
Attend to my prayer.
From the end of the earth I will cry to You,
When my heart is overwhelmed;
Lead me to the rock that is higher than I.
For You have been a shelter for me,
A strong tower from the enemy.
I will abide in Your tabernacle forever;
I will trust in the shelter of Your wings.

PSALM 61:1–4

Father,

We recognize that there are those who would speak evil against You when hardship knocks at their door. Let us forever stand firm in the foundation of our faith. Let us live in the center of Your will. We will come to You each day for strength and endurance. Help us, O God, to be the people You wish us to be, for we trust in You.

DAY 23

For You, O my God, have revealed to Your
servant that You will build him a house.
Therefore Your servant has found it in his heart
to pray before You. And now, LORD, You are
God, and have promised this goodness to Your
servant. Now You have been pleased to bless
the house of Your servant, that it may continue
before You forever; for You have blessed it,
O LORD, and it shall be blessed forever.

1 CHRONICLES 17:25–27

Lord,
We are so blessed that each day You come
to us with the gift of Your Spirit to help us
and strengthen our purpose for Your glory.
Continue to work in us, O Lord, and help
us grow to be the people You wish us to be.
Thank You for Your continued goodness
even when we stumble; thank You that You
are ever present to hold our hands and lift
us up. Your unconditional love has been
promised forever. Thank You for Your gracious mercy to us each day.

"Therefore I say to you, whatever things you ask when you pray, believe that you receive them, and you will have them. And whenever you stand praying, if you have anything against anyone, forgive him, that your Father in heaven may also forgive you your trespasses."

MARK 11:24–25

Father,
Help our nation with its unbelief! Lead us into a renewed relationship with You! Forgive us when we find fault in our brothers. Help us to look beyond their shortcomings and look deeper within ourselves to become better people. Forgive us when we fall short of doing all that You've called us to do, and when we fail to demonstrate love and forgiveness toward those who wrong us. Thank You for the blessing of knowing that we are forgiven—no matter what.

DAY 25

*Now it came to pass, as He was praying in
a certain place, when He ceased, that one of
His disciples said to Him, "Lord, teach us to
pray, as John also taught his disciples."*

LUKE 11:1

Lord,
We come to You with open hearts and ask
that You speak to our spirits with words
of wisdom and direction, that we may
know how You wish for us to pray. Help
Your humble servants to speak words
of praise and adoration, for You are the
King of kings and the Lord of lords. Teach
us, Lord, that we may know You and the
power of Your resurrection. Fill us with
Your presence and forgive our shortcomings. Lead us, O Lord, to a higher place,
that You might be lifted up and draw all
men to You.

John F. Kennedy

Let us therefore proclaim our gratitude to Providence for manifold blessings—let us be humbly thankful for inherited ideals—and let us resolve to share those blessings and those ideals with our fellow human beings throughout the world.

On that day let us gather in sanctuaries dedicated to worship and in homes blessed by family affection to express our gratitude for the glorious gifts of God; and let us earnestly and humbly pray that He will continue to guide and sustain us in the great unfinished tasks of achieving peace, justice, and understanding among all men and nations and of ending misery and suffering wherever they exist.

—Written for Thanksgiving Day 1963

DAY 26

Give ear to my prayer, O God,
And do not hide Yourself from my
supplication.
Attend to me, and hear me;
I am restless in my complaint, and moan
noisily.

PSALM 55:1–2

Lord,
There are so many times when we have
burdens almost too heavy to bear. Our
nation faces hardships and pain; we
need Your wisdom and help in all areas.
Strengthen us as a people and lead us in
the way that will bring honor and glory
to You. Lord, You have promised that if
we humble ourselves and seek Your face
and pray, You will heal our land. May we
forever be humble in Your sight, and may
we experience Your blessings in the midst
of our great need.

Cast your burden on the LORD,
And He shall sustain you;
He shall never permit the righteous to be
moved.

PSALM 55:22

Father,

You are so wonderful. Thank You for caring about our burdens. Open our hearts to Your Spirit and let us listen to Your voice. Strengthen us, O God, with confidence in You, that we may live for You and glorify Your name. Father, we praise You for all the gifts that You have given us. Draw us close to You that we may see Your glory.

DAY 28

The mouth of the righteous speaks wisdom,
And his tongue talks of justice.
The law of his God is in his heart;
None of his steps shall slide.

PSALM 37:30–31

Father,
True wisdom is a gift that only You, Father,
can give. May we always be in right stand-
ing with You. Let the words we speak
honor You, and let us never speak Your
name in vain. Let us stay steadfast and live
in such a way that Your light will shine
through us wherever we go. Thank You,
Father, for Your mercy and love.

*So Jesus answered and said to them,
"Assuredly, I say to you, if you have faith and
do not doubt, you will not only do what was
done to the fig tree, but also if you say to this
mountain, 'Be removed and be cast into the
sea,' it will be done. And whatever things you
ask in prayer, believing, you will receive."*

MATTHEW 21:21–22

O Lord,
Strengthen our faith. Help us to never
doubt Your Word or Your faithfulness. Lift
us up that we may boldly proclaim Your
truth each and every day. Let us be sensitive to the leading of Your Spirit and never
forget that "I can do all things through
Christ who strengthens me" (Philippians
4:13). Lord, we praise You because Your
mercies are new every morning, and Your
faithfulness is great.

DAY 30

Therefore, I exhort first of all that supplications, prayers, intercession, and giving of thanks be made for all men, for kings and all who are in authority, that we may lead a quiet and peaceable life in all godliness and reverence. For this is good and acceptable in the sight of God our Savior.

1 TIMOTHY 2:1–3

Lord,
Our nation needs Your guidance and direction. We humbly ask that Your Spirit intercede with the leaders of the nation, giving them the wisdom to make decisions that will honor You. We pray fervently for peace both here and abroad. Let us live with reverence for You and with peace in our hearts for our fellow man. We know this is Your desire. May we always remember that You are our God and Savior.

Ronald Reagan

To preserve our blessed land we must look to God. . . . It is time to realize that we need God more than He needs us. . . .

Let us, young and old, join together, as did the First Continental Congress, in the first step, in humble heartfelt prayer. Let us do so for the love of God and His great goodness, in search of His guidance and the grace of repentance, in seeking His blessings, His peace, and the resting of His kind and holy hands on ourselves, our nation, our friends in the defense of freedom, and all mankind, now and always.

The time has come to turn to God and reassert our trust in Him for the healing of America. . . . Our country is in need of and ready for a spiritual renewal. Today, we utter no prayer more fervently than the ancient prayer for peace on Earth.

"The Lord bless you and keep you; the Lord make His face to shine upon you and be gracious unto you; the Lord lift up His countenance upon you and give you peace. . . ." And God bless you all.

—FROM A SPEECH TO THE AMERICAN PEOPLE, FEBRUARY 6, 1986

Because Your lovingkindness is better than
  life,
My lips shall praise You.
Thus I will bless You while I live;
I will lift up my hands in Your name.
My soul shall be satisfied as with marrow
  and fatness,
And my mouth shall praise You with joyful
  lips.

PSALM 63:3–5

O Lord,
Let us never forget to praise Your holy
name. You are a wonderful God. You are
slow to anger and patient, with an unconditional love that has no end. Let us
bless You each day and lift up our thanks
in praise for the wonderful things You have
done for us. May we forever give honor
to Your name, for without You we are
nothing.

DAY 32

★
★ ★

*This Book of the Law shall not depart from
your mouth, but you shall meditate in it
day and night, that you may observe to do
according to all that is written in it. For then
you will make your way prosperous, and
then you will have good success.*

JOSHUA 1:8

Father,
You have given us a guide for life and have
asked us to meditate in Your Word day
and night. Place that desire within our
hearts—give us a hunger for Your Word,
that we may know You. Lord, You want us
to be successful in life and to be prosperous in all that we do. Lead us back to Your
Word that we may honor You through all
that we say and do.

How precious is Your lovingkindness, O God!
Therefore the children of men put their trust
  under the shadow of Your wings.
They are abundantly satisfied with the
  fullness of Your house,
And You give them drink from the river of
  Your pleasures.
For with You is the fountain of life;
In Your light we see light.

PSALM 36:7–9

Lord,
Your lovingkindness is new every day. May
we forever trust in You with all our hearts
and find rest in the shelter of Your love.
The very life we live comes from You alone.
Bless us, O Lord, with the light of Your
presence and place within us the desire to
share Your light so that others may come
to know the saving grace of our Lord and
Savior.

DAY 34

The Lord is my light and my salvation;
Whom shall I fear?
The Lord is the strength of my life;
Of whom shall I be afraid?
When the wicked came against me
To eat up my flesh,
My enemies and foes,
They stumbled and fell.
Though an army may encamp against me,
My heart shall not fear;
Though war may rise against me,
In this I will be confident.

PSALM 27:1–3

O Lord,
Today we face many hardships in a time when our faith is continually tested. But we know there is nothing to fear because You, Lord, are in control of all things. You are our strength and our defender; there is nothing too hard for You. Therefore, let us be confident in our faith and bold in telling others of Your marvelous unconditional love.

I will bless the LORD at all times;
His praise shall continually be in my mouth.
My soul shall make its boast in the LORD;
The humble shall hear of it and be glad.
Oh, magnify the LORD with me,
And let us exalt His name together.

PSALM 34:1–3

Lord,
You are the Creator of the universe—we praise Your blessed and holy name! You alone are the provider of all things, and with You all things are possible—may You always be lifted up! Let us live each day in the center of Your will and live for Your glory. If we say nothing, the rocks will cry out Your magnificent name. Let all men praise Your holy name, for You are a marvelous God, and Your light shines over all who choose to call You Lord.

DWIGHT D. EISENHOWER

Almighty God, as we stand here at this moment my future associates in the executive branch of government join me in beseeching that Thou will make full and complete our dedication to the service of the people in this throng, and their fellow citizens everywhere.

Give us, we pray, the power to discern clearly right from wrong, and allow all our words and actions to be governed thereby, and by the laws of this land. Especially we pray that our concern shall be for all the people regardless of station, race, or calling. May cooperation be permitted and be the mutual aim of those who, under the concepts of our Constitution, hold to differing political faiths; so that all may work for the good of our beloved country and Thy glory. Amen.

—FIRST ACT AFTER RECEIVING
THE OATH OF OFFICE,
JANUARY 20, 1953

Teach me Your way, O LORD;
I will walk in Your truth;
Unite my heart to fear Your name.
I will praise You, O Lord my God, with all
my heart,
And I will glorify Your name forevermore.

PSALM 86:11–12

Lord,
We hunger for Your Word. Teach us the
way that we should go and help us to walk
in Your truth each day. May Your praise
always be on our lips, and may You fill our
hearts with the joy of Your love and blessing. You are a gracious and loving God
whose mercy is new every morning.

DAY 37

I will bless the LORD who has given me
counsel;
My heart also instructs me in the night
seasons.
I have set the LORD always before me;
Because He is at my right hand I shall not be
moved.

PSALM 16:7–8

Father,
We humbly ask for Your blessing. Help
us to listen to Your counsel when we are
alone with You. Speak to our hearts each
moment, for You are the anchor of our
souls, and we will rest in Your presence. It
is You alone we desire, and no one or nothing can take Your place.

Blessed is the man
Who walks not in the counsel of the ungodly,
Nor stands in the path of sinners,
Nor sits in the seat of the scornful;
But his delight is in the law of the LORD,
And in His law he meditates day and night.
He shall be like a tree
Planted by the rivers of water,
That brings forth its fruit in its season,
Whose leaf also shall not wither;
And whatever he does shall prosper.

PSALM 1:1–3

Lord,
Your Word has given us counsel on how
we should relate to and act toward one
another. May we be steadfast and im-
movable in our commitment to You and
to one another. Let our roots go deep into
your Word to praise and glorify Your
name. May our weakness be Your strength
and our purpose in life be to honor You.

DAY 59

★
★ ★

Hear a just cause, O LORD,
Attend to my cry;
Give ear to my prayer which is not from
deceitful lips.
Let my vindication come from Your presence;
Let Your eyes look on the things that are
upright. . . .
Uphold my steps in Your paths,
That my footsteps may not slip.

PSALM 17:1–2, 5

Lord,
We cry out to You with hearts that need
Your blessings. Give us wisdom to make
right decisions that will bring honor to You
and will purify our hearts. Let the words
that we speak draw us closer to Your presence. We recognize, O Lord, that You are
in control of all things. Help this nation
to hear Your voice, protect us from evil,
and lead us in the path of righteousness for
Your name's sake.

*Let every soul be subject to the governing
authorities. For there is no authority except
from God, and the authorities that exist are
appointed by God. . . . Render therefore to
all their due: taxes to whom taxes are due,
customs to whom customs, fear to whom
fear, honor to whom honor.*

ROMANS 13:1, 7

Lord,
We live in a nation that is free to elect
those chosen for public office. We confess
that the servants who are chosen are there
with Your approval. Let us faithfully sup-
port those elected to office, giving honor
to their position. Let us help them fulfill
the obligation and responsibility for our
nation. With prayer and understanding,
let us unite ourselves to the one purpose of
living a life in which "In God We Trust."

PSALM 119:33–40

Teach me, O LORD, the way of Your statutes,
And I shall keep it to the end.
Give me understanding, and I shall keep
*   Your law;*
Indeed, I shall observe it with my whole
*   heart.*
Make me walk in the path of Your
*   commandments,*
For I delight in it.
Incline my heart to Your testimonies,
And not to covetousness.
Turn away my eyes from looking at worthless
*   things,*
And revive me in Your way.
Establish Your word to Your servant,
Who is devoted to fearing You.
Turn away my reproach which I dread,
For Your judgments are good.
Behold, I long for Your precepts;
Revive me in Your righteousness.

We the People

Tranquility, provide for the comm
erty, & ordain and establish this Co

All legislative Powers herein grante
tives.

The House of Representatives shall
shall have the Qualification
rson shall be a Repre
t not, when elected, be a
sentatives and direct
hich shall be determin
ree fifths of all othe
every subseque
sand, but each
have three; Ma
are one; Mary
en vacancies hap
House of Rep

3. The Senate o

The Great Awakenings

THE FIRST GREAT AWAKENING
1735–1745

The Great Awakening was a period in our history when revival spread throughout the colonies and people were drawn to prayer and a greater spiritual experience. This was a time when American colonies were questioning the role of the individual in their Christian walk and their role in society. This was a time of enlightenment, which emphasized the power of each individual to understand the approach to salvation and the power of prayer.

Great men such as Jonathan Edwards and George Whitefield were key Americans who preached for close to ten years in New England colonies with emphasis on the personal approach to religion. These men helped unify the American colonies and helped the Great Awakening spread through the work of numerous preachers and revivals. This movement fulfilled people's need for reassurance, direction, and religious purpose. People became united in the understanding of their Christian faith and life.

Jonathan Edwards

THE SECOND GREAT AWAKENING

The Second Great Awakening was a Christian revival movement during the early nineteenth century in the United States. It began around 1800 and gained momentum by 1820. The movement expressed a theology, by which every person could be saved through revivals. Many converts believed that the awakening heralded a new millennial age. This awakening stimulated the establishment of many reform movements designed to remedy the evils of society before the second coming of Jesus Christ.

During this time in history, church membership soared. The Methodist circuit riders and local Baptist preachers made enormous gains. In the newly settled frontier regions, the revival was implemented through camp meetings. Each camp meeting was a religious service of several days' length with multiple preachers. They were committed to individuals achieving a personal relationship with Jesus Christ.

The Second Great Awakening had a profound impact on American religious history. The membership numbers of the Baptist and Methodists grew dramatically during this period in history. The application of Christian teaching to social problems was commonplace during the early part of the nineteenth century.

Camp Meeting of the Methodists in N. America

THE THIRD GREAT AWAKENING

During the Third Great Awakening, religion played a dominant role in American history. Protestant denominations had a strong sense of social activism. They developed the post-millennial theology that the second coming of Christ would come after the entire earth had been reformed. Social issues gained momentum from the awakening, as did the worldwide missionary movement.

This was a time in history that the mainline Protestant churches were rapidly increasing in number. As the numbers grew, so did their wealth and educational levels. Focusing on reaching the unchurched in America and around the world, many built colleges and universities to train the next generation. In society, the role of a missionary was held in high regard.

Charles Finney